This book was compiled by Daniel Melehi
with the A.I assistance of Inventabot

<u>Dedication</u>

I hope this helps all of my wonderful
readers achieve all their goals in their
business. And I would like to thank my
wonderful wife for all of her continued
support in all my ventures.

May 7 2023

Contents

Introduction to Unity 8

Overview of the Unity interface 8

The Scene view...9

The Game view...9

The Hierarchy window 9

The Inspector window..10

The Project window..10

Understanding the Unity terminology 10

Game objects 11

Components 11

Prefabs 11

Scripts..11

Creating a new project in Unity 12

Overview of the Unity interface 12

Understanding the Unity Terminology...........................14

Game Development with Unity: From Beginner to

Professional 15

Chapter 1: Introduction to Unity 15

Subchapter 1.3: Creating a new project in Unity 15

Chapter 2: Understanding Game Development 16

Subchapter 2.1: Game design principles 17

Subchapter 2.2: Player experience and engagement 18

Subchapter 2.3: The role of game development tools.....19

Game Design Principles 20

Gameplay Mechanics 21

Game Balancing... 21

Player Motivation 21

User Experience (UX)... 22

Game Effects 22

Game Progression 22

Player Experience and Engagement............................**23**

The Role of Game Development Tools.....................**24**

Scripting in Unity **26**

Introduction to C# **26**

Data Types... 27

Variables.. 27

Functions 27

Basic Scripting in Unity **28**

Writing Your First Script 28

Manipulating Game Objects.. 28

Adding Game Mechanics.. 29

Advanced Scripting Techniques **29**

Optimizing Your Code... 29

Creating Reusable Scripts 30

Introduction to C# **30**

Basic Scripting in Unity.....................................**32**

Game Development with Unity: From Beginner to
Professional...**34**

Chapter 3: Scripting in Unity..............................**34**

Subchapter 3.3: Advanced scripting techniques 34

Chapter 4: Creating Game Objects in Unity **36**

Subchapter 4.1: Creating 2D game objects 36

Subchapter 4.2: Creating 3D game objects 37

Subchapter 4.3: Applying materials to game objects 38

Creating 2D Game Objects...39

Creating 3D Game Objects 41

    Step 1: Adding a 3D Object to the Scene.........................41

    Step 2: Modifying the Game Object 41

    Step 3: Adding Components...42

    Step 4: Combining Multiple Game Objects 42

Applying Materials to Game Objects 43

    Creating and Adding Materials...43

    Applying Textures..44

    Working with Shaders 44

    Conclusion 44

Chapter 5: Implementing Game Mechanics.................45

Subchapter 5.1: Physics in Unity..................................45

    Colliders and Rigidbodies 46

    Forces and Motion 46

Subchapter 5.2: Animation in Unity............................47

    Animation Basics 47

    State Machines and Layers..47

Subchapter 5.3: Audio in Unity....................................48

    Unity's Audio System...48

    Using AudioMixers in Unity 49

Subchapter 5.1: Physics in Unity..................................49

Animation in Unity 51

    Understanding Animation Clips...51

Setting Up Animation in Unity...52

Animation Controllers and States 52

Using Animation Events 53

Conclusion 53

Subchapter 5.3: Audio in Unity...................................**54**

User Interface Design in Unity **56**

Creating menus in Unity..**56**

Building responsive UI elements **57**

Navigation and user input **58**

Creating Menus in Unity..**59**

Building Responsive UI Elements................................**61**

Layout Optimization 61

Animations 62

Menus 62

Feedback 62

Conclusion 63

Navigation and User Input...**63**

Navigation 64

User Input...64

Conclusion 65

Chapter 7: Integrating External Assets into Unity........**66**

Subchapter 7.1: Importing assets into Unity..................**66**

Subchapter 7.2: Creating custom assets in Unity **67**

Subchapter 7.3: Working with asset bundles.................**68**

Importing Assets into Unity..**69**

Creating Custom Assets in Unity..................................**70**

Working with Asset Bundles...**72**

What are Asset Bundles? 72

Creating Asset Bundles..73

Using Asset Bundles 74

Conclusion 74

Chapter 8: Multiplayer Game Development in Unity....**75**

Subchapter 8.1: Overview of multiplayer game

development..**75**

Different Types of Multiplayer Game Modes.......................76

Tips for Creating Engaging Multiplayer Gameplay 77

Subchapter 8.2: Networking in Unity...........................**78**

High-Level Networking 78

Low-Level Networking...79

Subchapter 8.3: Creating Multiplayer Game Mechanics..**80**

Overview of Multiplayer Game Development **81**

Networking in Unity **83**

Subchapter 8.3: Creating Multiplayer Game Mechanics..**84**

1. Consider the game's objective 85

2. Balance gameplay for all players 86

3. Encourage Communication 86

4. Provide loads of rewards.................................86

5. Test and refine your game mechanics...................87

Chapter 9: Optimizing Your Game in Unity..................**88**

Subchapter 9.1: Understanding performance metrics in

Unity...**88**

Other performance metrics to consider:....................89

Subchapter 9.1: Understanding Performance Metrics in

Unity...**90**

6

Profiling and Optimization Techniques...........................92

Subchapter 9.3: Debugging Your Game in Unity 93

Chapter 10: Publishing Your Game................................*95*

Subchapter 10.1: Preparing for Publishing......................95

Subchapter 10.2: Publishing Options in Unity.................96

Subchapter 10.3: Promoting Your Game to the Targeted
Audience..97

Conclusion 98

Preparing for Publishing 98

Final Testing and Debugging 99

Optimizing Performance 99

Preparing Marketing Materials 100

Choosing a Platform 100

Preparing for Launch 101

Publishing Options in Unity 101

Introduction to Unity

Unity is a powerful game development tool that allows developers to create immersive and engaging gaming experiences. In this chapter, we will discuss the basics of Unity, including its interface, terminology, and how to create a new project.

OVERVIEW OF THE UNITY INTERFACE

When you first open Unity, you will be presented with a user interface that may seem overwhelming at first. However, once you become familiar with the interface, it becomes more intuitive and easy to use. The Unity interface is divided into several main windows, including the Scene view, Game view, Hierarchy window, Inspector window, and Project window.

The Scene view

The Scene view is where you will design and build your game environment. In this view, you can add game objects, lights, cameras, and other assets to create a 3D or 2D scene for your game.

The Game view

The Game view is where you can see your game as it will appear to the player. This view can be used to test gameplay mechanics, lighting, camera angles, and other aspects of your game.

The Hierarchy window

The Hierarchy window displays a list of all the game objects in your current scene. You can use this window to organize and manipulate game objects in your scene by changing their position, rotation, and scale.

The Inspector window

The Inspector window displays all the properties and components of a selected game object. You can use this window to modify the properties of game objects, add components, and adjust their values.

The Project window

The Project window is where you can manage all the assets and resources for your game, including scripts, textures, audio files, and more. You can create folders, import assets, and organize your project in this window.

UNDERSTANDING THE UNITY TERMINOLOGY

Unity has its own unique terminology that you will need to become familiar with in order to use the software effectively. Some of the most common terms used in Unity include game objects, components, prefabs, and scripts.

Game objects

Game objects are the fundamental building blocks of a Unity scene. They can represent anything from 3D models to lights to scripts that control gameplay mechanics.

Components

Components are individual parts of a game object that define its behavior and functionality. Examples of components include rigidbodies, colliders, and scripts.

Prefabs

Prefabs are pre-made game objects that can be reused throughout your game. They are commonly used for things like enemies, power-ups, and props.

Scripts

Scripts are code files that are used to define the behavior and functionality of game objects within Unity. They are written in

C#, Unity's scripting language, and are attached to game objects as components.

CREATING A NEW PROJECT IN UNITY

Creating a new project in Unity is a simple process. When you open Unity, select "New Project" and choose a name and location for your project. You can then select the 2D or 3D template, depending on the type of game you want to create. Once your project is created, you can start adding game objects, components, and scripts to create your game.

OVERVIEW OF THE UNITY INTERFACE

Unity is a powerful game development engine that provides developers with a wide range of tools to build games. The Unity interface is designed to be user-friendly and intuitive, making it easy for developers to navigate and create their games efficiently. When you open Unity for the first time, you will be greeted with the Unity Editor, which is the main interface used to create and edit Unity projects. The Editor is divided into several key areas, including the Scene View, Game View, Hierarchy window, and Inspector window. The Scene View is where you will be able to visually create and edit your game world, adding elements such as terrain, characters, and other objects. The Game View, on the other hand, provides a preview of what your game will look like when it is running. The Hierarchy window displays a list of all the objects in your scene, while the Inspector window provides detailed information and controls for each selected object. Unity also includes a range of additional windows, such as the Project window, which displays all the assets used in your project, and the Console window, which displays debug logs and error messages. As you become more familiar with the Unity interface, you will quickly learn how to use the various tools and features to create engaging games that stand out.

UNDERSTANDING THE UNITY TERMINOLOGY

To be able to use Unity effectively, it is essential to understand its terminology. This subchapter will define some of the most commonly used terms in Unity; **GameObject:** Everything displayed on the screen in Unity is contained within a GameObject. It is the primary object with which the user interacts. **Components:** Components are smaller parts of a GameObject that define certain attributes or functionalities of the object. For example, a SpriteRenderer component defines the image assigned to a 2D object. **Scene:** In Unity, a scene is a container that holds all the objects and components that make up a particular level or section of a game. **Assets:** Assets refer to any images, sounds, 3D models or other digital media used within a Unity project. **Inspector:** The

Inspector window shows the information and properties of any GameObject or Component selected in the Editor. **Hierarchy**: The Hierarchy window lists all objects within a scene. It provides a tree view of all objects present in a scene. **Project window**: The Project window contains all the files and folders included in a Unity project. By becoming familiar with these Unity-specific terms, you will be better equipped to create games effectively and efficiently.

Game Development with Unity: From Beginner to Professional

CHAPTER 1: INTRODUCTION TO UNITY

Subchapter 1.3: Creating a new project in Unity

Creating a new project in Unity is the first step towards developing your own game. In this subchapter, you will learn how to create a new project in Unity. When you open Unity, you will see the Unity Hub. This is where you can create new projects, open existing projects, and manage your Unity installations. To create a new project in Unity, follow these steps: 1. Click on the "New Project" button in the top right corner of the Unity Hub. 2. Give your project a name and choose a location to save it. 3. Select the template you want to use for your project. There are a number of different templates available, including 2D, 3D, and VR. 4. Choose the Unity version you want to use for your project. 5. Click the "Create" button to create your new project. Once your project is created, you will see the Unity Editor. This is where you will do most of your work when developing your game. In the next subchapter, we will take a closer look at the Unity interface and learn about the different windows and tools available to you.

Chapter 2: Understanding Game Development

Game development is an exciting process that requires a balance of creativity, technical skill, and attention to detail. In this chapter, we will explore the principles of game design, player experience, and the role of game development tools. By understanding these key concepts, you will be better equipped to create immersive and engaging games that keep players coming back for more.

SUBCHAPTER 2.1: GAME DESIGN PRINCIPLES

Game design is the process of creating the rules, mechanics, and overall experience that players will encounter in your game. It requires a deep understanding of what makes games fun and engaging, as well as the ability to balance competing priorities such as challenge and accessibility. One of the fundamental principles of game design is the concept of flow. Flow refers to the state of being fully immersed and engaged in an activity, to the point where time seems to fly by. To create flow in your game, it is important to find the right balance of challenge and skill. The player should feel challenged but not overwhelmed, and the game should offer a clear progression of difficulty as the player becomes more skilled. Another important principle of game design is understanding your target audience. Different types of games appeal to different types of players, so it is important to research and understand your audience before beginning development. Are you targeting hardcore gamers or casual players? What age group are you targeting? Is your game meant to be played on desktops or mobile devices? These are all important questions to consider when designing a game.

SUBCHAPTER 2.2: PLAYER EXPERIENCE AND ENGAGEMENT

Creating an engaging player experience is critical to the success of any game. This involves not only creating a fun and challenging game, but also creating a narrative and world that draws the player in. Storytelling is a powerful tool for creating immersion and engagement in your game. Another way to engage players is through the use of rewards and incentives. These can take many forms, from unlocking new levels or characters, to earning in-game currency or achievements. By offering meaningful rewards, you can keep players motivated and engaged throughout the game. Finally, it is important to consider the social aspects of gaming. Multiplayer games that allow players to connect and compete against each other can be incredibly engaging and add a whole new dimension to your game.

SUBCHAPTER 2.3: THE ROLE OF GAME DEVELOPMENT TOOLS

Game development is a complex process that requires a wide range of technical skills. Fortunately, there are many tools available to help simplify the process. One of the most popular game development tools is Unity, which we will be using throughout this book. Unity provides a powerful game engine, a user-friendly interface, and a range of built-in tools and resources for creating games. Another important tool for game development is version control. Version control software allows you to track changes to your code and assets over time, making it easy to collaborate with other developers and roll back changes if necessary. Other useful tools for game development include graphics editors such as Photoshop or Gimp, sound editors like Audacity, and programming tools such as Visual Studio or Atom. By leveraging the power of these tools, you can streamline your workflow and focus on creating great games.

GAME DESIGN PRINCIPLES

Game design is the process of creating the rules, mechanics, and aesthetics of a video game. Understanding game design principles is essential for game developers who want to create engaging and entertaining gaming experiences. Here are some key game design principles:

Gameplay Mechanics

Gameplay mechanics are the rules, systems, and interactions that make up the gameplay of a video game. They are the building blocks that allow players to move, interact, and progress through the game. Well-designed gameplay mechanics should be intuitive, challenging, and rewarding.

Game Balancing

Game balancing is the process of adjusting the gameplay mechanics to create a fun and engaging experience for players. It involves tweaking factors such as difficulty, pacing, and resource management to ensure that the game remains challenging without being frustrating.

Player Motivation

Player motivation refers to the reasons why players are interested in playing a game. It can be influenced by factors such as the game's storyline, characters, graphics, and mechanics. A well-designed game should provide clear goals and incentives that drive players to continue playing.

User Experience (UX)

User experience (UX) refers to the player's overall experience of interacting with the game. Key elements of UX include accessibility, ease of use, and engagement. A good UX will keep players engaged and immersed in the game world.

Game Effects

Game effects are the visual and audio elements that enhance the player's experience of the game. These include elements such as music, sound effects, visual effects, and animations. Well-designed game effects can greatly enhance the player's immersion in the game world.

Game Progression

Game progression refers to the process of moving through the game from beginning to end. It includes elements such as level design, pacing, and difficulty. A well-designed game progression should keep players motivated to advance through the game while presenting them with new challenges and rewards.

PLAYER EXPERIENCE AND ENGAGEMENT

Creating a successful game is not only about the technical aspects of making it, but also about the player's experience and engagement. The player's enjoyment of the game is what ultimately determines its success. One important aspect of creating a great player experience is ensuring that the game is easy to learn but difficult to master. This encourages players to keep playing and working to improve their skills. Additionally, having a well-designed tutorial or onboarding process can greatly improve the player's understanding of the game mechanics and how to play. Another key element of player engagement is the game's story or theme. A compelling story or engaging theme can help draw players into the game world and keep them interested. It can also give players a sense of purpose and motivation, making their overall experience more satisfying. The game's art and audio can also greatly impact the player's experience and engagement. Having high-quality graphics and immersive sound effects can help create a more compelling and immersive game world. It is important to ensure that these elements fit well with the game's overall theme and style. Overall, player experience and engagement should be a key consideration throughout the game development process. By prioritizing the player's enjoyment and satisfaction, developers can create games that are not only technically sound but also highly engaging and fun to play.

THE ROLE OF GAME DEVELOPMENT TOOLS

Game development tools are software programs that are essential for anyone interested in making video games. These tools can range from game engines that provide a framework for developing games, to asset creation tools that allow developers to build custom game assets such as 3D models, sprites, and sound effects. Unity is a powerful game development tool that provides an intuitive interface and a wide range of features that allow developers to create games that are both visually stunning and technically sound. It also provides a powerful scripting engine that allows developers to create game mechanics and artificial intelligence in a way that is easy to understand and modify. Other popular game development tools include Unreal Engine, GameMaker Studio, and RPG Maker. Each of these tools has its strengths and weaknesses, but they all provide a similar framework for developing games and a lot of support from a thriving community. In addition to game engines and asset creation tools, there are also tools for optimizing game performance, debugging, and testing. These tools are essential for ensuring that a game runs smoothly and without errors. Overall, game development tools are a crucial part of making video games. They provide a framework and support for developers to create immersive, engaging gameplay experiences that can captivate players for hours on end.

Scripting in Unity

Unity offers a robust scripting interface that allows game developers to implement custom game mechanics. Chapter 3 will introduce you to C# programming basics and show you how to use programming to make the games you want to make.

INTRODUCTION TO C#

Before you can start scripting inside Unity, you need to know the basics of C# programming. This subchapter will show you some fundamental programming concepts that you'll use in Unity, such as data types, variables, and functions.

Data Types

In C#, data types help the compiler understand what kind of data you're working with. Some common data types you'll use in Unity include integers, floats, booleans, and strings.

Variables

Variables are used to store data values in your program. They have a name and a data type, and you can assign and change their values as needed.

Functions

Functions are blocks of code that perform a specific task. You can call them when needed to execute that code. In Unity, functions are often used to update the state of game objects or to perform calculations.

BASIC SCRIPTING IN UNITY

Now that you have a basic understanding of C# programming, it's time to start scripting inside Unity. This subchapter will show you some simple examples of how to use scripting to manipulate game objects and add game mechanics.

Writing Your First Script

The first step in creating a script in Unity is creating a new file and adding some basic code. This subchapter will show you how to create a new C# script in Unity and how to attach that script to a game object in your scene.

Manipulating Game Objects

Once you have a script attached to a game object in your scene, you can use that script to manipulate the properties and transform of that game object. This subchapter will show you how to change the position, rotation, and scale of a game object using scripting.

Adding Game Mechanics

Now that you're comfortable manipulating game objects through scripting, it's time to add some game mechanics. This subchapter will show you how to create a simple game mechanic, such as moving a player character using input from the keyboard.

ADVANCED SCRIPTING TECHNIQUES

Once you're comfortable with scripting in Unity, you can start exploring more advanced techniques. This subchapter will show you how to optimize your code for performance and how to create reusable scripts that you can use in multiple projects.

Optimizing Your Code

Optimizing your code is an important part of game development, especially if you're targeting mobile devices or lower-end hardware. This subchapter will show you some tips and tricks for writing efficient code that runs smoothly on any device.

Creating Reusable Scripts

Creating reusable scripts can save you a lot of time and effort in your game development projects. This subchapter will show you how to create modular scripts that can be used in multiple projects, as well as how to create custom editor scripts that streamline your workflow.

INTRODUCTION TO C#

Before diving into game development with Unity, it is important to have a basic understanding of the programming language used in Unity: C#. C# is a widely used, powerful language that is easy to learn and offers developers the ability to create complex applications with ease. C# is an object-oriented programming language that is designed to work with Microsoft's .NET framework. It includes features such as garbage collection, type safety, and simplified type declarations, among others. These features make it one of the most popular programming languages for game development. To get started with C#, it's important to understand the basic syntax of the language. C# code is typically written in a text editor or an integrated development environment (IDE) such as Visual Studio. A C# program can consist of one or more classes, which contain definitions for variables, methods, and events. In C#, variables are declared using a type followed by a variable name, as seen in the following example: ```csharp int score; ``` This declares a variable named "score" with a type of "int", which stands for integer. C# also includes a wide range of language constructs, including loops, conditional statements, and object-oriented concepts such as interfaces and inheritance. These language constructs allow developers to create complex programs with ease.

Overall, C# is a powerful language that is essential for Unity game development. With a basic understanding of the language, developers can create complex and engaging games with ease.

BASIC SCRIPTING IN UNITY

Unity scripting is the core aspect of game development in Unity. Understanding Unity scripts and learning the basics is crucial to making games. C# is used in Unity scripting, making it an object-oriented language. In Unity, scripts are attached to game objects and are used to add behaviors to them. Basic scripting in Unity involves understanding the structure and syntax of C# programming language, as well as the components and properties of game objects. To get started with basic scripting in Unity, you need to have a basic understanding of C# programming. You should also understand the Unity interface and how to create game objects. Here are some key concepts to keep in mind when scripting in

Unity: - **Game Objects:** These are the visual entities in a Unity game. They can be anything from a simple cube to a complex character. - **Components:** These are the building blocks of game objects in Unity. They define the properties and behaviors of game objects. Examples of components include mesh renderers, colliders, and scripts. - **Functions:** Functions are blocks of code that perform specific actions. They are used to add behaviors to game objects. Examples of functions include Start(), Update() and OnCollisionEnter(). - **Variables:** Variables are containers for data. They can store numbers, strings, or references to objects. Variables are used to pass information between functions and to store data for later use. When scripting in Unity, start with simple scripts and build up your knowledge gradually. Practice writing scripts that affect the behavior of game objects. For example, you could create a script that moves a cube when the player hits a key, or a script that changes the color of an object when the player clicks on it.

Learning basic scripting in Unity is an essential part of becoming a game developer. With patience and practice, you can master the basics and create amazing games.

Game Development with Unity: From Beginner to Professional

CHAPTER 3: SCRIPTING IN UNITY

Subchapter 3.3: Advanced scripting techniques

In this subchapter, we will be exploring some advanced scripting techniques in Unity. These techniques will help you create more robust and efficient game code. One technique you can use is Object Pooling. This involves creating a pool of objects at the start of the game, and reusing them as needed. This improves performance by reducing the number of objects created and destroyed during gameplay. Another technique is Coroutines. These are functions that can be paused and resumed, allowing for more efficient, asynchronous code. You can use Coroutines to create timed events, animations, and more. A common optimization technique is Caching. This involves storing frequently accessed data in variables, to avoid constantly searching for the same data. This can greatly improve performance, especially for larger projects. Another advanced technique is Delegates. These are functions that can be passed as arguments to other functions. This allows for more flexible and reusable code, as you can swap out different functions without changing the original code. Finally, we will explore Reflection. This allows you to examine and modify code at runtime, which can be useful for debugging and fine-tuning your game. However, it should be used sparingly, as it can also impact performance. By utilizing these advanced scripting techniques, you can create more efficient and flexible game code, which will ultimately lead to a better player experience.

Chapter 4: Creating Game Objects in Unity

SUBCHAPTER 4.1: CREATING 2D GAME OBJECTS

Creating 2D game objects is straightforward in Unity. To get started, simply click on the "GameObject" menu in the Unity Editor and select "2D Object." This will display a dropdown menu of available 2D objects, including sprites, tile maps, and text meshes. Sprites are 2D images that can be used for characters, items, and backgrounds. They can be imported into Unity from external sources or created directly in the Unity Editor. To create a sprite in Unity, simply click on the "Create" menu in the Project window and select "Sprite." This will open the Sprite Editor, where you can draw your sprite using various tools and brushes. Tile maps are used to create 2D game environments by tiling together small images called tiles. To create a tile map in Unity, click on the "GameObject" menu and select "2D Object," then select "Tilemap." This will create a blank tile map that you can fill with tiles by clicking on them in the Tile Palette window. Text meshes are used to display dynamic text in 2D games. To create a text mesh in Unity, click on the "GameObject" menu and select "3D Object," then select "TextMeshPro - Text." This will create a 3D text object that you can position and resize in the Unity Editor.

SUBCHAPTER 4.2: CREATING 3D GAME OBJECTS

Creating 3D game objects in Unity is similar to creating 2D game objects. To get started, click on the "GameObject" menu and select "3D Object." This will display a dropdown menu of available 3D objects, including cubes, spheres, and cylinders. Cubes are the most common 3D object used in games for creating walls, floors, and other structures. To create a cube in Unity, simply click on the "Create" menu in the Project window and select "3D Object," then select "Cube." This will create a cube in the center of the scene that you can resize and move around. Spheres are used for creating rounded objects like balls and planets. To create a sphere in Unity, click on the "GameObject" menu and select "3D Object," then select "Sphere." Cylinders are used for creating objects like pipes, tunnels, and pillars. To create a cylinder in Unity, click on the "GameObject" menu and select "3D Object," then select "Cylinder."

SUBCHAPTER 4.3: APPLYING MATERIALS TO GAME OBJECTS

Materials are used to define the visual properties of game objects in Unity. A material can consist of a color, texture, and other settings like shininess and transparency. To apply a material to a game object, simply drag and drop the material onto the object in the Unity Editor. To create a new material in Unity, click on the "Create" menu in the Project window and select "Material." This will create a new material asset that you can customize by adjusting its properties in the Material Inspector window. You can also import materials into Unity from external sources like Photoshop or Blender. In addition to basic materials, Unity supports advanced shaders that can be used to create complex visual effects like reflections, refractions, and water surfaces. Shader programming requires knowledge of the Unity shader language and is typically used by experienced developers.

CREATING 2D GAME OBJECTS

Creating game objects is an essential part of game development in Unity. In this subchapter, we will be focusing on how to create 2D game objects. Unity provides several tools for creating 2D game objects, including the 2D sprites, which can be used to create basic shapes and characters. To create a new 2D game object, we can go to the GameObject menu and select 2D Object. We can then choose from several options, including Sprite, Text, and Tilemap. The Sprite option allows us to create a 2D image, which can be animated and set up as a character or environment object. We can import our sprites from external sources, or we can create them within Unity using the built-in Sprite Editor. Once we have created our 2D sprites, we can assign them to game objects by dragging and dropping them onto the Sprite Renderer component in the Inspector window. In addition to sprites, Unity also provides several other 2D objects, such as Text and Tilemap. Text objects can be used to display text on the screen, while Tilemaps can be used to create 2D environments and levels. In conclusion, creating 2D game objects in Unity is a straightforward process that can be done using the tools provided by the engine. By using the Sprite Editor, we can create dynamic and engaging 2D game objects that will enhance the player's gaming experience.

Creating 3D Game Objects

Creating 3D game objects is a crucial aspect of game development with Unity. 3D game objects not only give your game a visually appealing look but also provide a more immersive gameplay experience. To create a 3D game object in Unity, you need to follow these steps:

Step 1: Adding a 3D Object to the Scene

Firstly, you need to select "GameObject" from the top menu of the Unity editor and then select "3D Object." After that, you can select any of the following 3D objects: - Cube - Sphere - Capsule - Cylinder - Plane - Quad

Step 2: Modifying the Game Object

Once you have created a 3D game object, you can modify its properties to suit your game's needs. Some of the properties that you can change include: - Position - Rotation - Scale - Material - Texture - Lighting

Step 3: Adding Components

You can also add components to your 3D game object to give them some functionality. Some of the components that you can add include: - Collider: To give your game object the ability to interact with other game objects - Rigid body: To give your game object physics properties - Audio source: To add sound effects to your game object

Step 4: Combining Multiple Game Objects

You can combine multiple game objects to create more complex 3D models. Unity provides a feature called "Parenting" that allows you to group different game objects together. In conclusion, creating 3D game objects in Unity is a simple process that can bring your game to life. With a little bit of creativity and the right components, you can create visually appealing game objects that will keep your players engaged.

APPLYING MATERIALS TO GAME OBJECTS

Materials are an important part of game design, as they define how a game object's surface looks and interacts with light. Unity's Material component allows you to define the visual properties of a game object, including color, texture, and shading. In this subchapter, we'll explore the basics of applying materials to game objects in Unity.

Creating and Adding Materials

To create a new material, go to the Project panel and select "Create > Material". Unity will create a new material asset in your project folder. You can then drag and drop the material onto a game object's Material slot in the Inspector panel.

Applying Textures

Textures are images that are used to define a game object's surface appearance. To apply a texture to a material, simply drag and drop the texture asset onto the material's Texture slot in the Inspector panel. You can also adjust texture properties such as offset, tiling, and scaling.

Working with Shaders

Shaders are programs that define how a material responds to light and shadows in the game world. Unity includes a variety of built-in shaders that you can use to create different visual effects. To assign a shader to a material, you can select it from the Shader drop-down menu in the Inspector panel. You can also use custom shaders to define unique visual styles for your game.

Conclusion

Materials are a fundamental part of game design in Unity, allowing you to create visually appealing game objects with diverse surface appearances. By understanding the basics of materials, textures, and shaders, you'll be able to create stunning visual effects in your own projects.

Chapter 5: Implementing Game Mechanics

SUBCHAPTER 5.1: PHYSICS IN UNITY

In any game, physics plays an essential role in making the gameplay exciting and realistic. Unity offers a robust physics engine that can simulate various physical phenomena. With Unity's physics engine, you can easily create rigid and soft body simulations, gravity, collision detection, and more. You can also define and set up your own physical properties for game objects using colliders, rigidbodies, and joints. In this subchapter, we will go over the following topics:

Colliders and Rigidbodies

Colliders define the shape of game objects that interact with other colliders in the scene. Meanwhile, rigidbodies enable game objects to behave physically by simulating forces, torques, gravity, and collisions. In Unity, there are multiple types of colliders that you can use, including spheres, boxes, and capsules. You can also create your collider shapes using meshes.

Forces and Motion

In this section, we will learn how to apply different forces to Rigidbodies in Unity, which can make them move, rotate, and experience other physical effects. You can use the built-in physics system to apply forces such as torque, gravity, and velocity. We will also cover how to constrain the movement of Rigidbodies using joints.

SUBCHAPTER 5.2: ANIMATION IN UNITY

In game development, animations give life to game characters and components. With Unity, you can create complex and seamless animations that interact with the physics engine and control interface elements. In this subchapter, we will go over the following animation topics:

Animation Basics

Unity offers two types of animation systems: Legacy, and the newer Mecanim animation system. In this section, we will provide an introduction to Unity's animation tooling and explore how to create, manage, and play animations in Unity.

State Machines and Layers

Unity's Mecanim Animation system is built around the concept of State Machines that define how animations transition between one another. In this section, we will look closer at how to work with state machines and how to blend animations using Layers.

SUBCHAPTER 5.3: AUDIO IN UNITY

Audio is an essential aspect of game development that can set the mood for a scene and provide cues to indicate changes in the game's state. With Unity, you can easily incorporate sound effects and music into your game. In this subchapter, we will cover the following audio topics:

Unity's Audio System

Unity's audio system enables you to play various types of audio files, such as sound effects and music tracks. You can make use of 3D, spatial audio effects to give more immersiveness to your game environment. We will also cover the basics of scripting audio playback within your game development projects.

Using AudioMixers in Unity

AudioMixers allows you to set up complex audio processing, such as audio ducking, EQ adjustment, and downmixing. In this section, we will explore how to improve audio quality and structure audio playback within your game by leveraging AudioMixers.

SUBCHAPTER 5.1: PHYSICS IN UNITY

One of the most important aspects of game development is physics, and Unity provides a robust physics system that can be easily implemented into your game. The physics engine in Unity allows you to simulate realistic physical interactions between different game objects. To enable physics in your game, you will need to add a physics component to your game object. This can be done in the Unity inspector panel, under the "Add Component" button. Once you've added a physics component, you can set properties like mass, friction, and gravity scale to customize how the object will interact with other objects in the game world. Unity also provides a range of physics joints, which allow you to connect two game objects together and simulate realistic joint behavior. This can be useful for creating complex objects like vehicles or robots that need to move and interact with each other in a realistic way. One important feature of the Unity physics engine is the ability to use raycasts to detect collisions between objects. A raycast is a line that is cast out from a game object, and if it intersects with another object, you can trigger an event or perform some action. This can be used for things like detecting when a player character has collided with an enemy, or when a ball has hit a wall in a game of pinball. Overall, understanding how to use the physics engine in Unity is essential for creating engaging and realistic games that will keep players coming back for more.

ANIMATION IN UNITY

Animation is a crucial aspect of game development, and Unity offers a powerful animation system that can help create realistic and engaging game experiences. In this subchapter, we will dive into the basics of animation in Unity and cover some of the essential features that can be used to create compelling animations.

Understanding Animation Clips

In Unity, animation is achieved by using animation clips, which are individual animations that can be played on game objects like characters, props, and environments. Each animation clip consists of a series of keyframes that define the position, rotation, and scale of a game object at a particular point in time. These keyframes are interpolated in between to create smooth animations.

Setting Up Animation in Unity

To add animation to a game object in Unity, you must first create an animation clip. This can be done using the animation window, which provides a visual timeline editor for creating and manipulating animations. Once an animation clip has been created, it can be assigned to a game object's animator component, which will control how the animation is played.

Animation Controllers and States

In Unity, animation controllers are used to manage the transitions between different animation clips. An animation controller consists of a set of states, each of which is associated with a particular animation clip. Transitions can be set up between these states to define when one animation should start playing and when another should stop.

Using Animation Events

Animation events are a powerful feature of Unity's animation system that allow you to trigger code at specific points during an animation clip's playback. For example, you might use an animation event to play a sound effect when a character punches, or to spawn a particle effect when a projectile hits a surface. These events can be added to individual keyframes within an animation clip.

Conclusion

Animation is an essential aspect of game development and is crucial for creating engaging and immersive game experiences. In Unity, animation clips are used to define individual animations, while animation controllers and states are used to manage the transitions between them. By leveraging Unity's powerful animation system, game developers can bring their game worlds to life in ways that were previously only possible in their imaginations.

SUBCHAPTER 5.3: AUDIO IN UNITY

Audio is a crucial part of game development, as it helps to immerse the player in the game world and provides feedback for their actions. In Unity, there are various options for implementing audio in your game. One option is to use audio clips, which can be played back on game objects using an AudioSource component. Audio clips can be imported into Unity in a variety of formats, including MP3, WAV, and OGG. This allows for flexibility in implementing audio in your game, as you can choose the format that best fits your game's needs. Another option is to use the Unity Audio Mixer, which allows for more advanced audio processing and mixing. The Audio Mixer can be used to adjust volume levels, apply effects such as reverb and distortion, and create complex audio routing schemes. Unity also includes support for 3D audio, which allows for a more immersive audio experience. 3D audio simulates the way sound behaves in the real world, taking into account distance and direction. This makes it possible to create realistic spatial audio effects, such as sounds that appear to be coming from different directions in the game world. In addition to these options, Unity also supports integration with external audio middleware tools such as FMOD and Wwise. These tools provide even more advanced audio processing and mixing options, and can be used to create complex audio landscapes for your game. When implementing audio in your game, it's important to consider the overall sound design and how it fits into the game experience. Utilizing audio cues for important events or actions can help to reinforce the player's understanding of the game mechanics and increase engagement. It's also important to make sure that audio levels are balanced and not overwhelming for the player. In summary, Unity provides various options for implementing audio in your game, including audio clips, the Audio

Mixer, 3D audio, and integration with external audio middleware tools. Careful consideration of the overall sound design can help to create a more engaging and immersive game experience for players.

User Interface Design in Unity

CREATING MENUS IN UNITY

When it comes to creating menus in Unity, there are a few things to keep in mind. First, you'll want to consider the overall design of your user interface (UI). This includes things like the color scheme, font choice, and layout. Next, you'll want to think about the specific elements you'll include in your menus. Some common elements include buttons, sliders, and text fields. To create menus in Unity, you'll typically start by creating a new UI canvas. From there, you can add and arrange UI elements as needed. Unity provides a wide range of built-in UI components to choose from, as well as the ability to create custom UI elements using C#.

BUILDING RESPONSIVE UI ELEMENTS

One important aspect of UI design in Unity is ensuring that your UI elements are responsive. This means that they should look and function correctly across a range of different screen sizes and resolutions. To make your UI elements responsive, you can use Unity's anchoring and layout system. This allows you to specify how individual UI elements should be positioned and sized relative to the overall canvas. Another important consideration when building responsive UI elements is taking into account the aspect ratio of the user's screen. You can use Unity's aspect ratio fitter component to ensure that UI elements maintain their intended proportions across different screen sizes and resolutions.

NAVIGATION AND USER INPUT

In addition to the visual design of your UI, it's also important to consider the user's experience when actually interacting with your menus. This includes things like navigation and input. To create effective navigation in your menus, you can use Unity's built-in navigation system. This allows you to define a logical order for UI elements to be focused on when the user navigates using a keyboard or controller. For user input, it's important to consider the different input methods that may be available. This could include mouse and keyboard input or touch screen input on mobile devices. By designing your UI elements with different input methods in mind, you can ensure that your menus are accessible and easy to use for all users.

CREATING MENUS IN UNITY

Menus are a crucial part of any game, they provide an easy and intuitive interface for players to navigate through your game. Unity provides a flexible and customizable UI system that allows you to create menus that match the aesthetic of your game. To create a menu in Unity, you first need to select the Canvas object from the hierarchy window. The Canvas object is a basic component that allows you to create UI elements that can be rendered on screen. Once you have selected the Canvas, you can add UI elements such as Buttons, Text, Images, and Sliders to it. Buttons are a great way to create interactive elements in your menu. You can add a Button component to any GameObject by clicking on Add Component in the Inspector window and selecting UI -> Button. You can then customize the Button's appearance by changing its color, adding an image, or adjusting the size and position. Text elements can be added to your menu by adding the Text UI component to a GameObject. You can customize the font, size, and color of your text to match the aesthetic of your game. Images can also be added to your menu by adding the Image UI component to a GameObject and setting the image source. Unity also provides Layout Groups, which allow you to align and position UI elements in a flexible and adaptive way. You can use Layout Groups to ensure that your menu looks consistent across different screen sizes and resolutions. In conclusion, creating menus in Unity is a simple process that can have a significant impact on the overall user experience of your game. By utilizing Unity's flexible UI system, you can create menus that match the aesthetic of your game and provide an intuitive interface for players to navigate through your game.

BUILDING RESPONSIVE UI ELEMENTS

Creating a great user interface is key to engaging players. Responsiveness is an essential factor that makes or breaks the user experience. Responsive UI elements are those that quickly react and update when users interact with them. In this Subchapter, we'll look at some ways you can make your UI elements more responsive.

Layout Optimization

One practical way to enhance the responsiveness of your UI elements is through layout optimization. A well-organized layout should be intuitive to the user and support efficient navigation through the interface. The layout should also be optimized to work across different devices and resolutions, ensuring that UI elements provide the best user experience possible.

Animations

Animations can help add an element of life and interactivity that players find engaging. When used correctly, animations can improve the UX and attract more players. Animations can range from simple icon movements to complex character animations, and their execution depends on the specific game and its context.

Menus

Menus are significant UI elements that provide users with access to game functions and options. Ensuring that the menus are responsive can significantly boost engagement. Use simple, scalable menu systems to ensure that users can interact easily with the UI elements.

Feedback

User feedback is crucial to ensuring that the UI offers a positive experience. Incorporating feedback into UI elements, such as haptic responses or visual cues, can improve user immersion and engagement with the game.

Conclusion

A responsive user interface is essential to the success of any game. Incorporating layout optimization, animations, simple menus, and user feedback are significant ways to ensure that your UI provides the best experience possible. Remember, the UI is the bridge between the player and the game and investing in it will always be in your interest.

NAVIGATION AND USER INPUT

User Interface design is all about providing the best possible experience for the player. And to achieve that you need to ensure that navigation and user input in your game are intuitive and easy to use. In this subchapter, we will go over some best practices for creating effective navigation in your game as well as discuss how to handle user input.

Navigation

Navigation refers to how users move around your game. Good navigation should be easy to understand and streamline the player's experience. To create a good navigation system, you should consider the following:
- Keep it Simple: Keep the navigation simple and straightforward. Avoid adding unnecessary steps or inputs that can confuse or frustrate the player. - Use Familiar Elements: Use standard UI elements and patterns that your players will be familiar with. This makes it easier for players to understand how to move around and interact with your game. - Provide Feedback: Provide feedback to the player that shows where they are in the game and what they can do next. This can be done through labels, buttons, or even animations that indicate where the player should go.

User Input

User input is the way the player interacts with your game. It is important to design user input that is intuitive and easy to use. Here are some things to keep in mind when designing user input: - Limit the Buttons: Too many buttons can make it difficult for players to know where to look or what to do. Streamline the number of buttons and make sure they are easy to find and use. - Customize Controls: Allow players to customize their input controls so that they can play the game the way they want to. - Provide Feedback: Just like with navigation, it's important to provide feedback when players interact with your game. This can be done through animations, sound effects, or even vibrations.

Conclusion

Navigation and user input are crucial elements in game design. By creating a navigation system that is simple and easy to understand and designing user input that is intuitive and customizable, you can deliver a great user experience that keeps players engaged and coming back for more.

Chapter 7: Integrating External Assets into Unity

SUBCHAPTER 7.1: IMPORTING ASSETS INTO UNITY

Importing external assets into Unity is a crucial task in game development. Unity allows you to import a variety of asset types including images, audio, 3D models, and animations. Before importing any assets, it is important to ensure that they are compatible with Unity's file formats. This can be done by checking the supported file formats on the Unity website. To import an asset into Unity, first, select the 'Assets' panel in the Unity editor. From here, click on the 'Import New Asset' button and navigate to the asset file on your system. Once the asset is selected, Unity will automatically import and optimize it for use in your project. It is important to note that importing high-quality and large assets can impact the performance of your game. To mitigate this issue, Unity provides import settings that allow you to optimize assets to reduce their size without compromising their quality. These settings can be accessed by selecting the imported asset in the 'Assets' panel and adjusting its settings in the 'Inspector' panel.

SUBCHAPTER 7.2: CREATING CUSTOM ASSETS IN UNITY

Unity provides a range of tools that allow you to create custom assets within the editor. Some of these tools include the ability to create 3D models, animations, and graphics. To create a new asset, simply select the 'Assets' panel and click on the 'Create' button. From here, select the asset type you want to create and adjust its properties in the 'Inspector' panel. Unity also provides a range of plugins and extensions that can be used to create custom assets. These plugins often provide additional functionality and can significantly improve your workflow in Unity.

SUBCHAPTER 7.3: WORKING WITH ASSET BUNDLES

Asset bundles are a powerful feature in Unity that allow you to group assets together and load them asynchronously at runtime. This feature is particularly useful for optimizing game performance as it enables you to load only the assets that are required by a specific level or scene. To create an asset bundle in Unity, first, select the assets you want to include in the bundle and select 'Build Asset Bundle' from the 'Assets' menu. Once the bundle is built, it can be loaded into your game at runtime using the 'AssetBundle.LoadFromFile()' or 'AssetBundle.LoadFromMemory()' functions. It is important to note that asset bundles can significantly improve performance but can also complicate your project's architecture. It is recommended that you carefully plan and organize your assets before using this feature to avoid any issues later on in development.

IMPORTING ASSETS INTO UNITY

Importing assets into Unity is a fundamental part of game development. It's the process of bringing in 3D models, textures, music, and other media into your project. Unity supports a wide range of file formats, including .FBX, .OBJ, .WAV, and .MP3, among many others. To import an asset into your project, you can simply drag and drop the file into your Unity project window. Once Unity recognizes the file format, it will automatically generate an asset file for you that you can then add to your scene. Unity also includes a built-in Asset Store, which hosts thousands of free and paid assets. From environmental assets to character models, the Asset Store has a vast library of resources that you can utilize in your projects. It's important to note that when importing assets into Unity, you'll likely need to tweak the settings to optimize the asset for your specific project. This may include adjusting materials, texture settings, and mesh colliders to ensure that the asset works as intended in your scene. By importing high-quality assets into your project, you can enhance the visual and audio experience for your players and create a more immersive game world. In the next subchapter, we'll discuss how to create custom assets in Unity.

CREATING CUSTOM ASSETS IN UNITY

Unity provides a wide range of built-in assets to help developers create high-quality games, but sometimes you need something specific that is not available out-of-the-box. In such cases, you can create your own custom assets using Unity's built-in tools. Custom assets are essentially Unity objects such as models, textures, audio clips, or scripts that you create and save in your project. This allows you to reuse and share them within your own project as well as with others in the Unity Asset Store. To create a new custom asset in Unity, follow these steps: 1. Choose the type of asset you want to create. You can do this by selecting the Assets > Create menu option or by right-clicking in the Project window and selecting Create. 2. Select the type of asset you want to create from the pop-out menu. For example, if you want to create a new material, select Create > Material. 3. Give the asset a name and click on the Create button. This will add the new asset to your project. 4. Customize your asset by using Unity's built-in tools. For example, if you created a new material, you can now adjust its color, texture, and other properties. 5. Save your asset by pressing Ctrl+S or by selecting File > Save from the main menu. This will ensure that you don't lose any of your changes. In addition to creating new assets from scratch, you can also modify existing assets in Unity. This can be useful if you want to make small adjustments to a built-in asset without having to recreate it from scratch. Overall, creating custom assets in Unity is a powerful way to extend the functionality of the engine and create high-quality games with unique, customized content.

WORKING WITH ASSET BUNDLES

Unity allows game developers to create and distribute asset bundles. Asset bundles are a great way to package game assets and make them available to load at runtime. This helps to reduce build sizes and optimize game performance. In this subchapter, we'll discuss how asset bundles work and how to create and use them in your Unity projects.

What are Asset Bundles?

Asset bundles are collections of game assets that are packaged together for distribution. Asset bundles can include anything from textures, models, audio files, animations, and more. These bundles are then downloaded at runtime and used to enhance the gameplay experience. Asset bundles are especially useful when your game has a large number of assets that aren't all required for every level or area of your game. With asset bundles, you can load only the required assets for each level or area, which helps to reduce memory usage and improve game performance.

Creating Asset Bundles

To create an asset bundle in Unity, you'll first need to select the assets you want to include in the bundle. You can do this by selecting the assets in the Project window and choosing "Create Asset Bundle" from the context menu. Unity will then create a new asset bundle for you, which you can customize with different options like compression and encryption. Once you've created an asset bundle, you can include it in your game using Unity's built-in asset bundle management system. You can load asset bundles at runtime using the AssetBundle.LoadFromFile() method, which will load the asset bundle into memory and make its contents available for use in your game.

Using Asset Bundles

To use an asset bundle in your game, you'll first need to load it at runtime using the AssetBundle.LoadFromFile() method. Once the asset bundle is loaded, you can access its contents using the LoadAsset() method, which will load a specific object from the bundle. One of the main benefits of using asset bundles is that they allow for dynamic asset loading, which can greatly improve the performance and memory usage of your game. By only loading the required assets for each level or area, you can ensure that your game runs smoothly on a wide range of devices.

Conclusion

Asset bundles are a powerful feature of Unity that can greatly improve the performance and memory usage of your game. By packaging assets together and loading them dynamically at runtime, you can optimize your game for a wide range of devices and ensure that it provides an engaging and immersive experience for your players. In the next chapter, we'll discuss multiplayer game development in Unity, including networking, synchronization, and more.

Chapter 8: Multiplayer Game Development in Unity

SUBCHAPTER 8.1: OVERVIEW OF MULTIPLAYER GAME DEVELOPMENT

Multiplayer games offer an interactive experience that can engage players for hours. In Unity, you can develop multiplayer games with ease. Multiplayer game development involves creating a network-enabled game that can run on multiple devices with each device displaying the same information about the game. In multiplayer game development, you will need to learn about how to create the game mechanics in a way that is synchronized across all of the devices. This subchapter introduces you to the different types of multiplayer game modes and gives you tips on how to create engaging gameplay.

Different Types of Multiplayer Game Modes

There are different types of multiplayer game modes that you can create in Unity: - Cooperative: This mode involves two or more players working together to complete a specific objective. For example, in a game like "Left 4 Dead," four players work together to survive a zombie apocalypse. - Competitive: This mode involves two or more players competing against each other to see who comes out on top. For example, in a game like "Overwatch," two teams compete to complete specific objectives. - Hybrid: This mode combines cooperative and competitive modes, allowing players to work together and compete with each other at the same time. For example, in a game like "Fortnite," players can team up to survive and build, but they also need to fight against other players to be the last one standing.

Tips for Creating Engaging Multiplayer Gameplay

To create an engaging multiplayer game, you need to focus on making the gameplay fun, challenging, and rewarding. Here are some tips: - Balance the game: Make sure that the game is fair and balanced for all players. Avoid giving too much power to one player or team, as this can lead to toxicity and resentment. - Provide clear objectives: Make sure that players know what the objectives are and how to achieve them. This can help prevent frustration and confusion. - Build social features: Provide features that allow players to interact with each other, such as social networks and voice chat. This can help create a sense of community and enhance the gameplay experience. - Test, test, and test again: Make sure that the game is thoroughly tested before releasing it to the public. This can help identify and fix any bugs or glitches that could ruin the gameplay experience.

SUBCHAPTER 8.2: NETWORKING IN UNITY

In Unity, you can create a multiplayer game with the built-in networking system. Networking is a way to send messages between multiple devices so that they are all displaying the same information about the game. Unity offers two types of networking: - High-Level Networking: This is used for simple games that don't require a lot of custom code. It is easy to use but is not as flexible as the Low-Level Networking. - Low-Level Networking: This is for more complex games that require custom code. It allows you to create a custom networking solution that is tailored to your game's specific needs.

High-Level Networking

Unity's High-Level Networking system is based on the concept of authoritative servers. The authoritative server is responsible for keeping track of the game's state and sending the necessary updates to all connected clients. In High-Level Networking, you don't need to write a lot of custom code. Unity provides a lot of features out of the box that make it easy to create a basic multiplayer game. However, it may not be suitable for large or complex projects.

Low-Level Networking

Unity's Low-Level Networking system provides you with full control over the networking code. You can create a custom networking solution that is tailored to your game's specific needs. In Low-Level Networking, you need to write custom code for sending and receiving messages. This requires a good understanding of networking concepts and protocols. However, it gives you more flexibility to create advanced multiplayer games.

SUBCHAPTER 8.3: CREATING MULTIPLAYER GAME MECHANICS

Creating multiplayer game mechanics requires careful planning and execution. You need to make sure that the game mechanics work well in a multi-device environment and that there are no synchronization issues. Here are some tips for creating multiplayer game mechanics: - Use prediction: Prediction is a technique used to smooth out the gameplay experience. It involves predicting what a player will do next and then taking action on that prediction. This can help reduce latency and make the game feel more responsive. -

Synchronize game state: Make sure that all devices are displaying the same information about the game. This involves synchronizing the position of game objects and their states. - Handle network disconnections: Handle network disconnections seamlessly to prevent players from experiencing unexpected behavior in the game. - Implement anti-cheating measures: Implement measures to prevent cheating, such as validating player actions on the server. In the next subchapters, we'll delve deeper into the different types of networking in Unity.

OVERVIEW OF MULTIPLAYER GAME DEVELOPMENT

Multiplayer games have become increasingly popular, allowing players from different locations to connect and play together. As a game developer, it's important to understand the basics of multiplayer game development and the challenges it presents. Multiplayer game development requires creating a network infrastructure within the game to allow players to communicate with each other over the network. This involves concepts such as synchronization of game states across clients, handling latency and lag, and ensuring that the game runs smoothly for all players. Games can have different types of multiplayer modes such as co-op, versus, or massively multiplayer online (MMO) games. Each of these modes requires different approaches and programming techniques to create a fully functional multiplayer experience. One of the key aspects of multiplayer game development is designing the gameplay to ensure that it is suitable for multiplayer. Games that are designed for single-player may not translate well to multiplayer, and thus require significant adaptation to work smoothly in a multiplayer environment. Another challenge when developing multiplayer games is testing and debugging. With multiple players connected, issues such as synchronization and network lag can be difficult to diagnose and fix. It's important to test the game under a range of network conditions to ensure that it runs smoothly for all players. In the next subchapter, we'll be discussing networking in Unity and how it can be used to create multiplayer games.

NETWORKING IN UNITY

When it comes to creating multiplayer games, networking is a critical component in Unity. Unity has a built-in networking system called UNet, which allows developers to create multiplayer games easily. UNet uses a client-server architecture, where one player hosts the game as the server, and other players connect to the server as clients. Networking in Unity involves sending messages between the server and clients, such as player positions and game states. Developers must ensure that their game can handle synchronization issues and network latency to prevent players from experiencing lag or synchronization discrepancies. They must also manage server authority, which determines which player's input affects the game state. Unity provides several tools and techniques to manage networking, including Remote Procedure Calls (RPCs), which allow the server to call a function on the client and vice versa. Developers can also use network views to synchronize game objects over the network without having to write custom networking code. While networking in Unity may seem complex at first, with the right knowledge and tools, developers can create engaging multiplayer experiences for their players.

SUBCHAPTER 8.3: CREATING MULTIPLAYER GAME MECHANICS

Multiplayer gaming has become an essential component of modern video game development. Creating dynamic and challenging multiplayer game mechanics requires significant thought and planning. In this subchapter, we will explore how to create engaging multiplayer game mechanics in Unity. First, it is essential to understand the types of multiplayer gaming available. You can develop games that rely on client-server architecture or peer-to-peer architecture. In client-server architecture, a central server manages the game logic and data, while clients communicate with the server about the actions and status of the game. In contrast, in peer-to-peer architecture, each player communicates directly with other players, and there is no central server. To create effective multiplayer game mechanics, there are a few key principles to consider. First, you need to develop mechanics that encourage players to work together towards a common goal. You also need to design mechanics that make gameplay exciting and challenging for all players. Finally, you should consider how players will communicate and coordinate to achieve success. Here are some essential tips to consider when designing multiplayer game mechanics:

1. Consider the game's objective

When designing multiplayer mechanics, it is essential to consider the game's objective and what players need to do to succeed. You should design challenges that require teamwork and cooperation to be overcome. For example, you could create challenges that require players to coordinate attacks or defend one another.

2. Balance gameplay for all players

Multiplayer games need to be balanced to ensure everyone has an equal chance of success. You should strive to create mechanics that cater to diverse play styles, and provide players with unique experiences, regardless of their skill levels.

3. Encourage Communication

Effective communication is essential in multiplayer games. Ensure your game mechanics require and reward effective communication between players. You could offer in-game voice chat or text chat to make communication easier.

4. Provide loads of rewards

Rewarding players with prizes such as items or special abilities for accomplishing goals encourages continued gameplay and motivates users to do their best. You could award players for solving puzzles or obstacles, among others.

5. Test and refine your game mechanics

Testing and refining game mechanics are essential to ensure your game is challenging, balanced, and enjoyable. Playtest your game with a small group of beta testers to see what areas may require improvement or adjustment. With these tips in mind, you'll be able to develop multiplayer game mechanics that engage your players and provide a fun and challenging gaming experience.

Chapter 9: Optimizing Your Game in Unity

SUBCHAPTER 9.1: UNDERSTANDING PERFORMANCE METRICS IN UNITY

Optimizing your game is a crucial step before launching it. There are several things that can affect a game's performance, including graphics, physics, and audio. In Unity, there are a few performance metrics you can use to measure and improve your game's performance. One of the most important performance metrics in Unity is the FPS (frames per second). FPS is the number of frames that are rendered by Unity every second. A higher FPS means a smoother and more responsive game. To view your game's FPS, you can use the Unity profiler, which provides real-time data on your game's performance. Another important performance metric is the CPU usage. CPU usage is the amount of processing power that is being used by your game. If your game is using too much CPU, it can cause lag and slow down the game. Unity profiler can also provide data on your game's CPU usage. GPU usage is another important metric to consider. GPU usage is the amount of processing power that is being used by your graphics card. If your game is using too much GPU, it can cause overheating and even damage the graphics card. Unity profiler can also show you data on your game's GPU usage.

Other performance metrics to consider:

- Memory usage: the amount of RAM that is being used by your game.

- Draw calls: the number of times Unity sends a command to the graphics card to render an object on the screen.
- Batches: the number of objects that are being rendered together in a single draw call.

By understanding these performance metrics, you can identify the areas of your game that need improvement. In the next subchapter, we will discuss how to optimize your game using profiling and optimization techniques.

SUBCHAPTER 9.1: UNDERSTANDING PERFORMANCE METRICS IN UNITY

As a game developer, it is essential to understand the performance metrics in Unity. Performance metrics refer to the measurements that are used to evaluate the performance of your game in terms of speed, efficiency, and resource usage. One important performance metric to keep in mind is the frames per second (FPS). FPS refers to the number of frames that are displayed in one second. The higher the FPS, the smoother and more responsive the game will feel to the player. Generally, a good FPS for a game is around 60, but this may vary depending on the type of game. Another important performance metric is the draw calls. Draw calls refer to the number of objects that are being rendered on the screen at any given time. The more draw calls there are, the more strain it puts on the computer's graphics card, which can lead to a decrease in performance. It is important to optimize your game to reduce the number of draw calls. Memory usage is also a crucial performance metric to keep track of. Memory usage refers to how much memory your game is using at any given time. The more memory your game uses, the higher the chances of it crashing or lagging. It is important to optimize your game to reduce memory usage. Finally, CPU usage is another performance metric to keep in mind. CPU usage refers to how much of your computer's processing power your game is using. If your game uses too much CPU, it can slow down other processes on your computer and lead to lag or crashes. Understanding these performance metrics is essential to create a smooth and responsive game that engages players. In the next subchapter, we will discuss profiling and optimization techniques that you can use to improve the performance of your game.

PROFILING AND OPTIMIZATION TECHNIQUES

Optimizing your game is crucial for ensuring the best possible experience for players. Profiling can help you identify performance bottlenecks in your game by analyzing the memory usage and processing time of each frame. To start profiling your game, you can use Unity's built-in profiler, which provides a detailed breakdown of the performance of your game. This tool shows you how much time is spent on each aspect of your game, such as rendering or physics calculations. After identifying performance bottlenecks, you can begin optimizing your game. This can include reducing the number of draw calls, improving the efficiency of your code, or reducing the size of game assets. One useful optimization technique is to use a level-of-detail (LOD) system. This system reduces the detail of objects as they move further away from the player, reducing the workload on the GPU. You can also optimize your game by using batching, which combines multiple objects into a single draw call. This can reduce the number of draw calls required and improve performance. It is important to remember that optimizing your game should not come at the expense of the player experience. Always aim for a smooth and engaging gameplay experience, even if it means sacrificing some optimizations.

SUBCHAPTER 9.3: DEBUGGING YOUR GAME IN UNITY

Debugging is an essential part of game development that allows developers to identify and fix any issues that may arise during the development process. Unity provides developers with a powerful set of debugging tools that can help them troubleshoot their games and ensure that they are running smoothly. One of the most important debugging tools in Unity is the console window. The console window displays any errors, warnings, or informative messages that are generated by the game engine or scripts. Developers can use the console window to identify and fix any issues that may be preventing their game from running correctly. Another powerful debugging tool in Unity is the debugger. The debugger allows developers to set breakpoints in their code and step through it line-by-line to identify and fix any issues. With the debugger, developers can inspect variables, watch expressions, and track program flow to gain a deep understanding of how their game is working. In addition to the console window and debugger, Unity also provides developers with a range of other debugging tools, including the profiler, which can help developers identify performance issues, and the Unity Test Runner, which allows developers to create and run automated tests to ensure that their game is functioning correctly. When debugging a game in Unity, it is important to stay organized and focused. Developers should start by identifying the specific issues that they are trying to address and then work methodically to resolve them. By taking a structured approach to debugging and using the powerful debugging tools provided by Unity, developers can identify and fix any issues that may arise and ensure that their game is running smoothly.

Chapter 10: Publishing Your Game

Once you've finished creating your game with Unity, it's time to get it out there for people to play! In this chapter, we'll cover the necessary steps to prepare for publishing, the publishing options available in Unity, and how to effectively promote your game to your target audience.

SUBCHAPTER 10.1: PREPARING FOR PUBLISHING

Before your game can hit the market, there are a few important steps you need to take to prepare it for publishing. First, ensure that your game is functioning correctly and that all bugs have been fixed. Next, determine which platforms you will publish your game on and tailor your game to meet the requirements of each platform. Also, ensure that your game is visually appealing and represents your intended theme and audience. Lastly, you'll need to make sure that you meet all legal requirements such as registering your company, obtaining any necessary licenses, and protecting your game using copyright or trademark protection.

SUBCHAPTER 10.2: PUBLISHING OPTIONS IN UNITY

Unity offers a variety of publishing options to distribute your game on different platforms. You can choose to release your game on desktop platforms such as Windows, Mac, and Linux, on mobile platforms such as iOS and Android, or even on game console platforms such as Xbox, PlayStation, and Nintendo Switch. Unity provides built-in tools for each platform to help you package and deploy your game on your targeted platforms. Additionally, Unity offers several publishing licenses such as the Unity Plus and Unity Pro licenses that include more advanced features and options to expand your game development opportunities.

SUBCHAPTER 10.3: PROMOTING YOUR GAME TO THE TARGETED AUDIENCE

After you've published your game, it's important to promote it to your target audience to gain popularity and increase downloads. Take advantage of social media platforms to announce and advertise your game and showcase its features and functionality. Reach out to gaming websites and bloggers to write reviews or host giveaways to promote your game. Work on building a community around your game by engaging with your players and listening to their feedback to improve the game, and don't forget to regularly update your game with new content to keep players engaged.

Conclusion

Publishing your game can be just as exciting as developing it. Take the necessary steps, choose the right publishing options, and promote your game to your target audience to ensure its success. With Unity, you have all the tools you need to create an outstanding game and release it to the world.

PREPARING FOR PUBLISHING

Before you can release your game to the world, you need to prepare it for publishing. This involves several critical steps to ensure that your game is ready for distribution and that it will meet the expectations of your target audience. In this subchapter, we'll take a closer look at what you need to do to prepare your game for publishing.

Final Testing and Debugging

The first step in preparing your game for publishing is to perform final testing and debugging. This process involves thoroughly testing the game to identify any remaining bugs or issues and addressing them before release. You should test the game on multiple devices and platforms to ensure that it works smoothly across all of them.

Optimizing Performance

Another critical step in preparing your game for publishing is optimizing its performance. This involves identifying the areas of your game that are resource-intensive and finding ways to optimize them so that your game runs smoothly on all types of devices. Some of the best ways to optimize performance include reducing the number of draw calls, optimizing textures, and minimizing the use of expensive effects.

Preparing Marketing Materials

Once your game is thoroughly tested and optimized, it's time to start working on your marketing materials. These materials should include a compelling trailer video, high-quality screenshots and images, and a detailed description of the game's features and gameplay. You'll also need to create a press kit that includes additional assets such as logos, icons, and promotional images.

Choosing a Platform

When it comes to publishing your game, you have many options to choose from. You can release your game on popular platforms such as Steam, the App Store, or Google Play. You can also choose to self-publish your game on your website or through other distribution channels. Each platform has its own set of requirements and guidelines, so it's important to do your research and choose the best platform for your game.

Preparing for Launch

Finally, you'll need to prepare for the official launch of your game. This involves setting a release date, creating a press release, and sending out review copies to journalists and bloggers. You should also create a plan for promoting your game on social media and other marketing channels to build anticipation and generate buzz. By following these steps, you'll be well on your way to preparing your game for publishing and launching it successfully to the world.

PUBLISHING OPTIONS IN UNITY

After all the hard work put into creating your game in Unity, it's time to share it with the world. Publishing your game can be a daunting task, but Unity makes it easier with a variety of publishing options. Unity provides several ways to publish your game depending on your target platform: PC, Mac, mobile devices, and consoles. One of the most popular platforms for indie game developers is Steam, and Unity has made it easier to publish your game on this platform by providing seamless integration. Unity's platform-specific modules allow you to deploy and publish your game to different platforms. You can create standalone desktop applications for PC and Mac, or mobile apps for iOS and Android. Unity also provides support for consoles such as Xbox One and PlayStation 4. For PC games, you can publish your game on a variety of digital distribution platforms such as Steam, GOG, and itch.io. Unity allows you to create a standalone executable or use its integrated software installer to distribute your game. For mobile games, Unity provides a range of publishing options. You can publish your game on the Apple App Store or Google Play Store. Unity also allows you to export your game to a variety of mobile devices, including iPhones, iPads, and Android· phones and tablets. For console games, publishing requires additional steps. Unity allows you to build your game for specific consoles and then submit it to the respective console manufacturer's development portal for certification. Once approved, your game will be available on the console's digital storefront. In addition to these options, Unity also allows you to publish your game on the web. You can use WebGL to export your game to HTML5, which can then be played in a web browser. Unity also provides cloud-based hosting services such as Unity Cloud Build, which allows you to automate the building and publishing process. Overall, Unity provides a wide range of publishing options that cater to the needs of game developers. Whether you are targeting PC, mobile, or console platforms, Unity has got you covered. So get ready to share your creation with the world and watch it take flight!

www.ingramcontent.com/pod-product-compliance
Lightning Source LLC
Chambersburg PA
CBHW070423220526
45466CB00004B/1515